D0760860

APR 0 8

OUR BODY

Digestive System

Cheryl Jakab

Smart Apple Media

This edition first published in 2006 in the United States of America by Smart Apple Media.
Reprinted 2007

Smart Apple Media
2140 Howard Drive West
North Mankato
Minnesota 56003

First published in 2006 by
MACMILLAN EDUCATION AUSTRALIA PTY LTD
15–19 Claremont Street, South Yarra, Australia 3141

Visit our Web site at www.macmillan.com.au

Associated companies and representatives throughout the world.

Library of Congress Cataloging-in-Publication Data

Jakab, Cheryl.
   The digestive system / by Cheryl Jakab.
   p. cm. — (Our body)
   Includes index.
   ISBN-13: 978-1-58340-737-0
   1. Digestion—Juvenile literature. 2. Gastrointestinal system—Juvenile literature. I. Title.

QP145.J362 2006
612.3—dc22   2005057881

Edited by Ruth Jelley
Text and cover design by Peter Shaw
Illustrations by Guy Holt, Jeff Lang (p. 4 (bottom), pp. 5–6, p. 18),
   and Ann Likhovetsky (p. 30)
Photo research by Legend Images

Printed in USA

Acknowledgments
The author and the publisher are grateful to the following for permission to reproduce
copyright material:

Front cover photograph: Colored SEM/scanning electron micrograph of villi on the wall of
the small intestine, courtesy of Photolibrary/Eye of Science/Science Photo Library.
Front cover illustration by Jeff Lang.

© Peter E. Smith, Natural Sciences Image Library, p. 8; Photodisc, p. 22; Photolibrary/
Foodpix, pp. 14, 29; Photolibrary/Science Photo Library, pp. 10, 13, 16, 24, 26, 27, 28; Sarah
Saunders, p. 20.

Contents

Glossary words
When a word is printed in **bold**,
you can look up its meaning
in the Glossary on page 31.

Amazing body structures

The human body is an amazing living thing. The structures of the body are divided into systems. Each system is made up of **cells**. Huge numbers of cells make up the **tissues** of the body systems. Each system performs a different, vital function. This series looks at six of the systems in the most familiar living thing to you—your body.

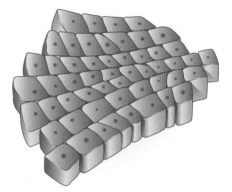

Cells make up tissues of the body systems.

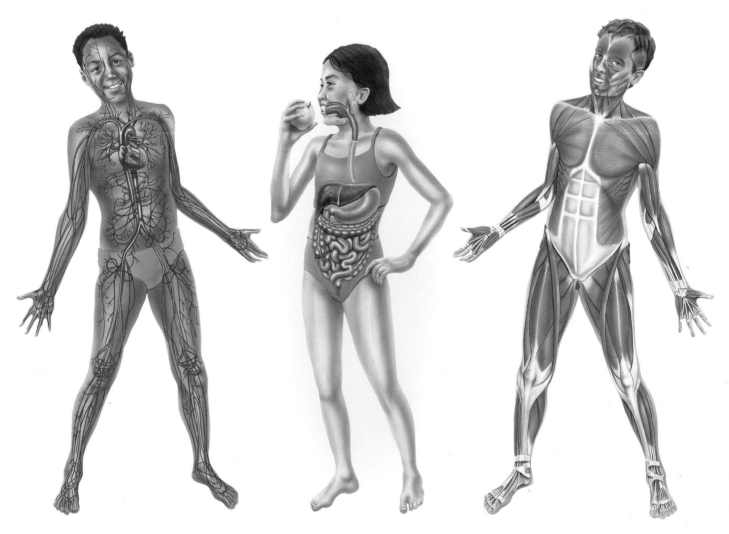

circulatory system   digestive system   muscular system

The digestive system

The digestive system processes food and provides energy and **nutrients** for the body. How much do you know about your digestive system?

- What happens to the food you swallow?
- What does each type of food do for your body?
- What happens when you vomit?
- What does it look like inside the digestive system?

This book looks at the human digestive system to answer these questions and more.

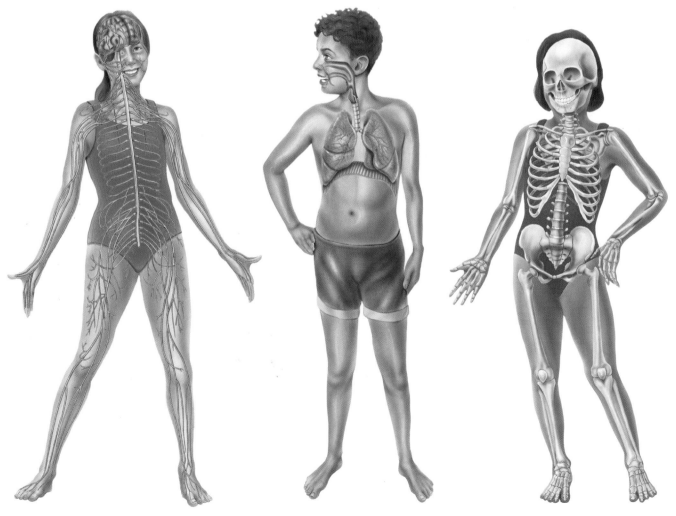

nervous system   respiratory system   skeletal system

Parts of the digestive system

There are two main parts of the digestive system:

- the **digestive tract,** from the mouth to the anus
- the **digestive organs,** which produce digestive juices.

You and your digestive system

You are very aware of many of the demands of your digestive system. You cannot ignore the feeling of hunger for long. Your digestive system signals what it needs and you respond.

FASCINATING FACT
The whole digestive tract in humans is about 33 feet (10 m) long.

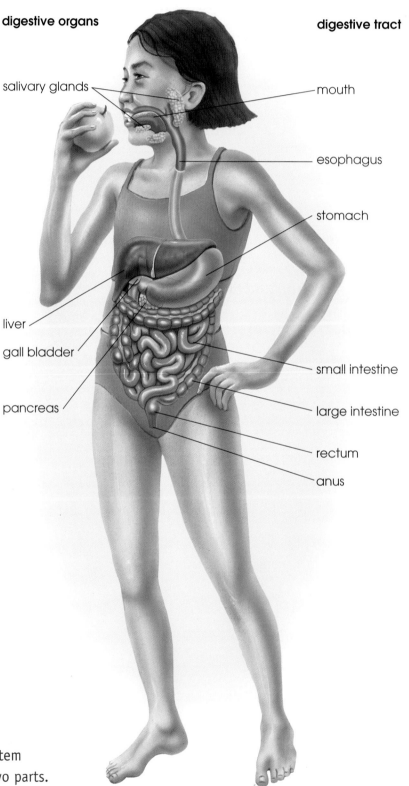

digestive organs

digestive tract

salivary glands

mouth

esophagus

stomach

liver

gall bladder

small intestine

pancreas

large intestine

rectum

anus

The digestive system is divided into two parts.

The digestive tract

The digestive tract creates a path for food to follow. It consists of many parts:

- the mouth, which is a chamber containing the tongue and teeth
- the esophagus (say e-sof-a-gus), which is a strong muscular tube running from the mouth to the stomach
- the stomach, which is a wide stretchy bag that sits below the oesophagus on the left side of the body
- the small intestine, which is a narrow but long tube that sits curled up in the middle of the **abdomen**
- the large intestine, which is a wide channel that sits around the small intestine

The digestive organs

The digestive organs are connected to the digestive tract, but they are not part of it. They produce juices which help break down foods in the digestive tract.
The digestive organs include:

- three pairs of salivary glands
- the pancreas
- the liver
- the gall bladder

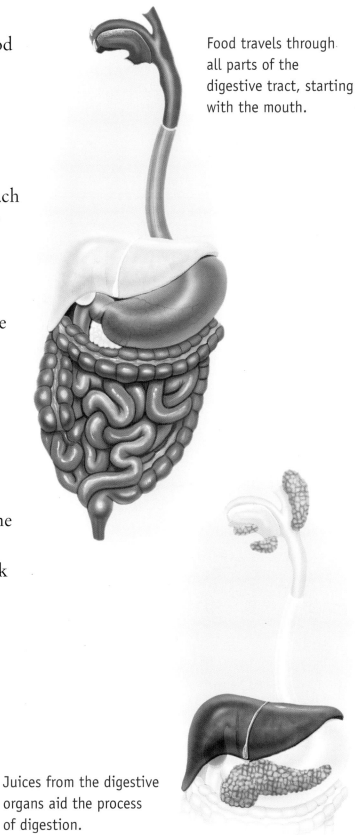

Food travels through all parts of the digestive tract, starting with the mouth.

Juices from the digestive organs aid the process of digestion.

Parts of the digestive tract

Each part of the digestive tract contributes to the process of digestion. Some parts break down the food, other parts absorb nutrients from the food matter into the bloodstream.

The mouth

In the mouth, food is chewed and saliva is added. The teeth, which cut and grind the food, are made of hard bone-like material called dentine. The teeth in different parts of the mouth have different shapes. Teeth at the front of the mouth are used for cutting and those at the back of the mouth are used for grinding. Saliva is a digestive juice that turns food into a soft, wet lump called a bolus. The tongue helps with mixing and swallowing food by pushing the bolus backward.

The surface of the tongue is covered by sense organs called taste buds. There are five main flavors that taste buds react to: sweet, salty, acid, bitter and umami (say oo-ma-mi). Umami is a savory flavor which was identified in 1908 by a Japanese researcher. Umami means "tasty" or "delicious" in Japanese.

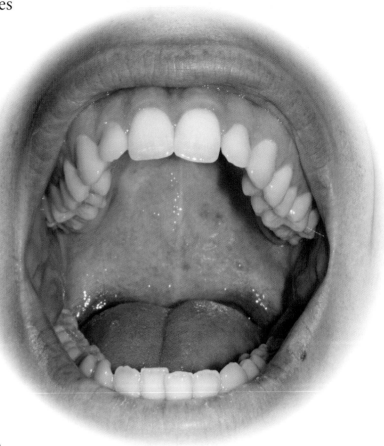

The processing of food begins in the mouth.

Foods and flavors

Different foods have different flavors, which are detected by the taste buds.

Flavour	Foods
sweet	sugar
salty	salt
acid	vinegar, lemon
bitter	grapefruit
umami	MSG, meat, cheese, tomatoes

The esophagus

Once the bolus leaves the mouth it moves down the esophagus. The esophagus is a tube with a smooth lining. Muscles in the wall of the esophagus push the bolus toward the stomach. At the lower end of the esophagus is a strong ring of muscle just above the stomach, called a sphincter. The sphincter separates the esophagus from the stomach.

The stomach

The stomach is a hollow sac shaped like the letter J. It has sphincters at each end which hold the bolus in the stomach while it is processed. The bolus is mixed with juices from the stomach wall to turn it into a smooth slurry, called chyme. Muscles in the stomach wall churn the chyme.

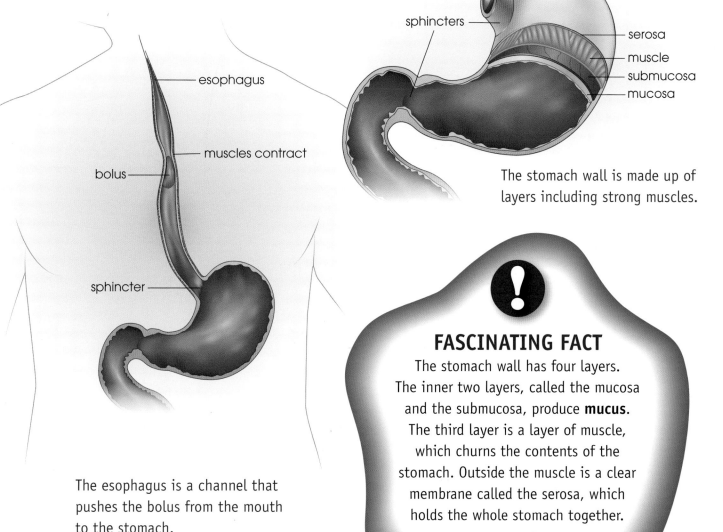

sphincters — serosa
muscle
submucosa
mucosa

The stomach wall is made up of layers including strong muscles.

esophagus

muscles contract

bolus

sphincter

The esophagus is a channel that pushes the bolus from the mouth to the stomach.

! FASCINATING FACT
The stomach wall has four layers. The inner two layers, called the mucosa and the submucosa, produce **mucus**. The third layer is a layer of muscle, which churns the contents of the stomach. Outside the muscle is a clear membrane called the serosa, which holds the whole stomach together.

The intestines

The chyme passes into the intestines after it has been processed by the stomach. The intestines are divided into two main sections: the small intestine and the large intestine. These two parts look very different to each other.

Small intestine

The small intestine lies in coils in the center of the lower abdomen. The small intestine is called "small" because it is a narrow tube, but it is actually very long. If it were stretched out it would be about 16 feet (5 m) long. The first part of the small intestine, which joins the stomach, is called the duodenum.

stomach

large intestine

small intestine

The small intestine sits under a fatty layer in the abdomen.

Villi
UNDER THE MICROSCOPE

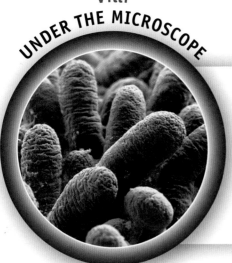

The walls of the small intestine have many finger-like projections, called villi. There are millions of these villi lining the small intestine.

Large intestine

The large intestine, also known as the bowel, is the last section of the digestive tract. It is a wide tube which sits around the small intestine. It has three sections, the caecum (say see-kum), colon, and rectum.

- The caecum is a short pouch that connects the small and large intestines.
- The colon is the main length of the large intestine. It runs up the right side of the abdomen, across the middle, and down the left side.
- The rectum is a short tube about 5 inches (12 cm) long at the end of the digestive system.

FASCINATING FACT

Near where the small and large intestines meet at the caecum, there is a small finger-like organ called the appendix. The appendix has no known function in humans.

transverse colon

ascending colon

caecum

appendix

rectum

descending colon

The colon is divided into three sections.

Organs that help digestion

The digestive organs produce juices that aid the process of digestion. These digestive juices contain **enzymes** that are necessary for the breakdown of foods.

Salivary glands

The salivary glands in the mouth produce saliva, which contains the enzyme ptyalin. Ptyalin begins the process of breaking down **starches**.

Pancreas

The pancreas is a small, grainy looking organ that sits behind the stomach. It produces powerful juices that are released into the small intestine to help break down food. It also releases a chemical into the intestines to weaken the effect of stomach acid.

stomach

large intestine   pancreas

TRY THIS

Neutralizing stomach acid

The contents of the stomach are acidic. Bicarbonate of soda is the chemical the pancreas secretes to neutralize stomach acid.

Mix an acid, such as vinegar, with bicarbonate of soda and see what happens.

The liver is a large wedge-shaped organ that is divided into two lobes, or sections.

The liver

The liver is the largest internal organ. It sits next to the stomach in the abdomen. The liver is the body's major chemical processing organ. It stores an energy source called glycogen as well as iron and some vitamins. The liver also produces digestive juice.

The gall bladder

Digestive juice is carried from the liver to a bag-like organ called the gall bladder. The juice in the gall bladder, together with waste from the liver, make up a digestive juice called bile. Bile is stored in the gall bladder until needed. It helps digest fats in the small intestine.

Liver cells UNDER THE MICROSCOPE

lobule

Liver cells process nutrients in the blood. They are arranged in groups around blood vessels. These groups of liver cells, called lobules, are about 0.4 inch (1 cm) wide.

Digestion

Digestion makes the energy and nutrients from food available to the body. Digestion involves:

- the physical breakdown of food by the teeth
- the chemical breakdown of nutrients for the body to absorb
- absorption of nutrients
- removal of what is eaten that cannot be digested

Each part of the digestive system has a different role in the digestive process.

✚ HEALTH TIP

Brush your teeth!

Plaque, which contains **bacteria**, builds up on tooth surfaces after eating sugary foods. The bacteria produce acids that eat into the teeth. Plaque needs to be removed regularly to keep teeth healthy.

Tip: Brush your teeth morning and night and have regular dental check-ups.

Physical breakdown

The physical breakdown of food begins in the mouth where it is chewed and mixed with saliva. Soft food, such as mashed potato, only needs to be chewed for a few seconds. Hard or tough food, such as meat, takes longer to chew and break down.

After chewing, small lumps of food, called boluses, are swallowed. They then travel down to the stomach through the esophagus. They are pushed along by a muscle action called **peristalsis**.

Digestion begins when food is chewed in the mouth.

Chemical breakdown

Food is broken down further by chemicals in digestive juices. Food is mixed with digestive juices in the mouth, stomach, duodenum, and small intestine.

In the mouth, the ptyalin in saliva starts breaking down starches into sugars. The bolus is swallowed and passes to the stomach.

The stomach secretes acid which helps break down **protein** and fat and kill bacteria. The bolus is mixed with this acid for a few hours and churned into a thin watery slurry, called chyme. The chyme is then passed on to the duodenum.

Bile from the the gall bladder is squirted into the duodenum to mix with the chyme. Juices from the pancreas also enter the small intestine. These juices contain many enzymes which break down the fats, proteins, and **carbohydrates** that the body needs into small molecules. The chyme then spends about two hours traveling through the small intestine, where the broken down nutrients are absorbed into the bloodstream.

!

FASCINATING FACT
Vomiting is the body's way of getting rid of unwanted material. Normally, food only passes downward through the digestive system, but when you vomit it comes back up. Vomiting can be caused by food poisoning or overeating.

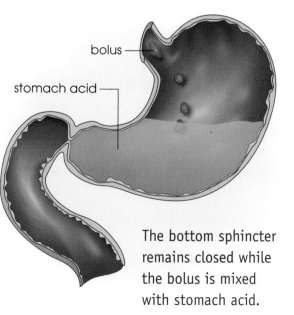

bolus

stomach acid

The bottom sphincter remains closed while the bolus is mixed with stomach acid.

sphincter opens

chyme

duodenum

The bottom sphincter opens to release the chyme into the duodenum.

Absorption of nutrients

The small intestine is where most of the nutrients are absorbed into the bloodstream. Small molecules of fats, proteins, and carbohydrates that have been broken down by enzymes pass into the bloodstream through the wall of the small intestine.

The nutrients are carried in the bloodstream to the liver where they are processed to make an energy source for the body. The liver stores this energy source and releases it when the body needs it.

Villi in the small intestine absorb nutrients, which then pass into the blood vessels.

**Bacteria in the colon
UNDER THE MICROSCOPE**

There are billions of bacteria in the colon which aid digestion, such as the pink cells shown here.

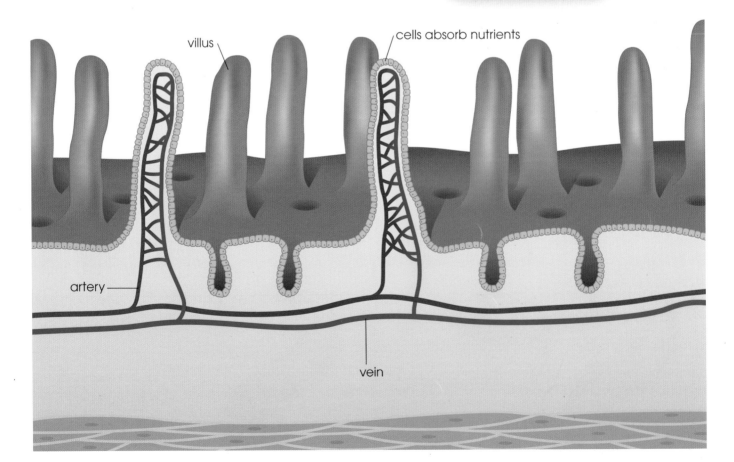

villus

cells absorb nutrients

artery

vein

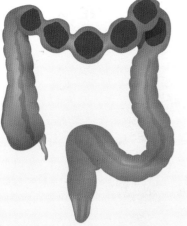

Water is absorbed from the waste.

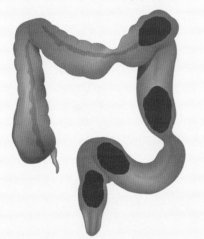

Waste is moved towards the rectum.

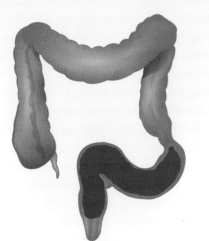

Waste collects in the rectum, ready to be eliminated.

Waste becomes solid as it passes through the large intestine.

Waste

Waste is what remains after food has been broken down and nutrients have been absorbed. The chyme that enters the large intestine is a mixture of waste and water. Waste enters the caecum after passing through the small intestine. The caecum connects to the colon, where waste travels slowly. It can take anything from ten hours to several days for waste to travel through the colon. The waste becomes more solid in the colon as water and salts are absorbed through the intestine wall.

When the lower part of the large intestine becomes full, the muscles work to push out the solid material, called feces. The solid waste moves through the rectum, which is usually kept empty except when waste is being eliminated.

TRY THIS

Digestion time

It usually takes about one day for food to pass through the digestive tract. But this time can vary greatly.

Find out how long your system takes by eating some easily identified food, such as licorice. Time how long it takes for the food to come out as waste.

Changes in the digestive system

Humans, like all mammals, feed their babies on milk produced in the mother's body. As the baby's digestive system develops, it becomes able to process other types of food.

Feeding before birth

Before birth a baby's developing digestive system is not in use. The baby gets all its nutrients and energy from its mother's body. The baby's blood circulation does not pass through the liver or the digestive system. Energy and nutrients are processed in the mother's body and passed on to the baby through an organ called the placenta.

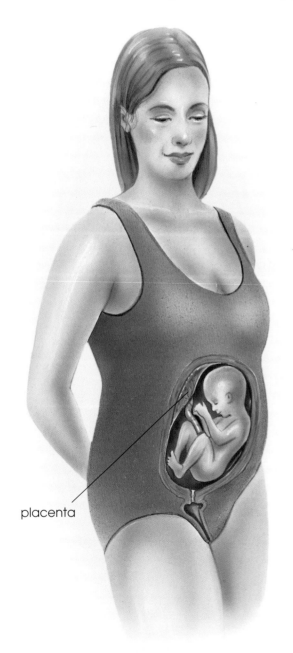

placenta

The baby receives all its nutrients through the placenta.

! FASCINATING FACT

Scientific studies have shown that the foods a mother eats while she is pregnant are more likely to be accepted by her children when they are older. The smells of foods that children were given during early childhood can trigger happy memories later in childhood.

Feeding after birth

After birth a baby's digestive system begins to function. At this time, breast milk is the most suitable food for the baby. It provides all the nutrients the baby needs and also protects the baby against infections. It is important that other foods are not added to the baby's diet before the developing body is ready to digest them.

Teeth

Humans have two sets of teeth in their lifetime. Most babies are born without teeth. The first teeth start to come through when a baby is around six months old. The first teeth are called milk teeth, or deciduous teeth. The deciduous teeth fall out and are replaced by second teeth, or adult teeth, in late childhood.

!

FASCINATING FACT

If a baby cannot be fed breast milk, "formula" can be used instead. This is an artificial alternative that is formulated on natural breast milk. It is important to have this alternative available if breastfeeding is not possible.

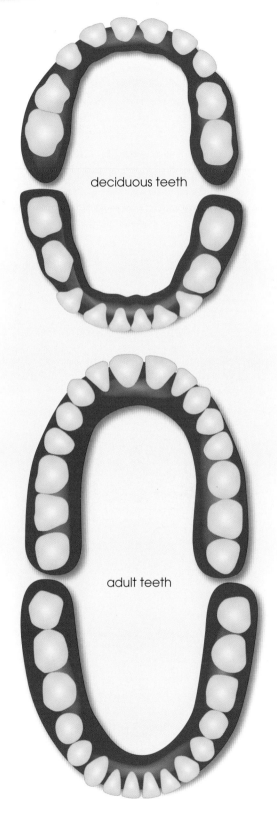

deciduous teeth

adult teeth

Deciduous teeth fall out as adult teeth grow in their place.

Establishing diet

Establishing a baby's diet is done over time as the digestive system develops. Breastfeeding continues for a few months, or sometimes years, as other foods are added to the diet. When the baby grows deciduous teeth and other parts of the digestive system mature, a variety of foods can be introduced to their diet.

Introducing solids

The introduction of foods other than milk to young children is a gradual process. Opinions on when foods should be introduced differ between cultures. Some people introduce solid food, such as soft cereal, when babies are as young as four months old. Other people delay this until much later.

FASCINATING FACT
The first bowel motion of babies after birth is a very black sticky substance called meconium. The bowel motions of breast-fed babies are a pale colour. They only start to be smelly when other foods are eaten.

A baby can begin to eat solid foods when its first teeth start to grow.

Frequency of body wastes

Young babies may have one or more bowel motions a day and will urinate many times. Initially there is no control over when this occurs. Slowly, the waste elimination decreases in frequency, particularly at night. Eventually it develops into a regular daily pattern for most children by school age or earlier.

Urinary system

The urinary system is completely separate from the digestive system. Urine is waste filtered from the blood that must also be eliminated regularly. Urine is formed in the kidneys and is then passed into the bladder. When the bladder fills we feel the need to empty it and must go to the toilet.

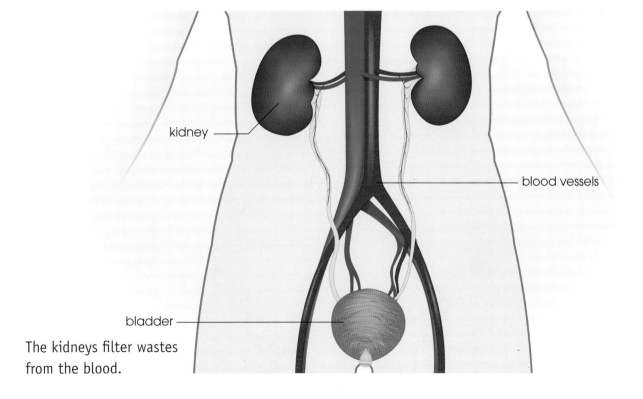

kidney

blood vessels

bladder

The kidneys filter wastes from the blood.

Digestive health

A good diet keeps the digestive system healthy. Digestive health normally depends on two main factors:

- energy from food should be equal to energy used by the body
- the food eaten must provide a balance of nutrients.

Energy from diet

The amount of energy required from the diet varies with activity levels. Growing children and teenagers require more energy than adults.

As food is digested, energy from the food is absorbed into the body. The energy content of food is measured in kilojoules or calories. One calorie equals 4.2 kilojoules. A young person needs about 8,200 kilojoules (2,000 calories) of energy intake per day.

Energy from foods

Scientists have discovered how much energy can be gained from eating different foods.

Type of food	Amount of energy
1 ounce of carbohydrates	0.11 calories
1 ounce of pure protein	0.11 calories
1 ounce of pure fat	0.23 calories

The energy from food is stored in the body and then used as required for all the body's activities

HEALTH TIP
Heartburn

Many people suffer heartburn after eating large meals. This feeling is actually food coming back up from the stomach past the oesophageal sphincter. This can happen when the sphincter is weakened or because the stomach is too full.

Tip: Never overfill your stomach by eating too much.

Nutrients in foods

People enjoy eating food but the energy and nutrients that food provides are more important than enjoyment. The main nutrients in food are proteins, carbohydrates, and fats. Meats, fish, and eggs provide protein to build body tissues. Carbohydrates in bread and fruits provide energy. Fats and oils are vital for the brain and nerves. Small amounts of chemicals called vitamins and minerals are also essential for a healthy body.

Water in the body

Approximately two-thirds of the human body is water, so it is important to have enough water in the diet. Eating a lot of fresh fruits and vegetables can provide much of the water that the body needs every day.

Nutrient	Source	Needed for
vitamin A	green and yellow vegetables	normal growth and good eyesight
vitamin B complex	meats, mushrooms	production of energy
vitamin C	citrus fruits, broccoli	blood clotting, tissue repair, healthy teeth and gums
vitamin D	egg yolk, liver, tuna	regulating the absorption of other minerals
vitamin E	seed oils and wheatgerm	may be involved in healing and protecting against cell damage
vitamin K	leafy green vegetables	blood clotting
iron	red meat, green leafy vegetables	red blood cells
calcium	cheese, yogurt	bones
phosphorus	seafood	cell functions, membranes
zinc	most foods	important in forming enzymes

Digestive problems

Digestive problems can be caused by poor nutrition or eating foods that contain harmful bacteria. Parts of the digestive tract can become blocked or develop an **ulcer** and cause pain. Treatment for severe problems may require surgery.

Dangerous micro-organisms UNDER THE MICROSCOPE

A common cause of food poisoning is the presence of dangerous **micro-organisms** in the food. Salmonella is a common micro-organism that causes food poisoning.

Digestive conditions

There are a range of conditions that can affect the digestive system.

Condition	Cause	Symptom	Treatment
diabetes	lack of **insulin** due to damage in the pancreas or a **genetic disorder**	blood sugar levels not maintained	injection of insulin, limit the amount of sugars in the diet
coeliac disease	genetic disorder affecting the intestines	unable to digest foods containing gluten, a substance found in processed flour	stop eating foods that contain gluten
hepatitis	infection of, or damage to, the liver	ranges from acute illness to inability to digest, skin becomes yellow in colour	treatment depends on the cause, control the intake of fats
gallstones	formation of stone-like crystals in the gall bladder	pain if the stones move into the small tubes leading to the small intestine	surgery to remove the stones from the tubes, reduce fat in the diet
appendicitis	swelling and inflammation of the appendix	pain in the lower left abdomen	surgery to remove the appendix
food poisoning, or "gastro"	eating food or drinking water that contains harmful bacteria	vomiting, **diarrhea**	stop eating, drink plenty of water, hospitalization if symptoms are severe

Dietary problems

Dietary problems, such as nutritional disorders, can be caused by not eating enough food. Eating the wrong foods or too much food can also lead to problems. Eating disorders, such as overeating and under eating, are becoming more common in developed countries where food is plentiful. Disorders that lead to under eating, such as anorexia nervosa and bulimia, are caused by an intense fear of gaining weight or becoming severely overweight.

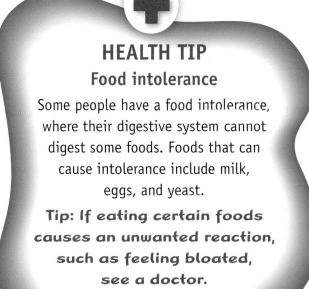

HEALTH TIP
Food intolerance

Some people have a food intolerance, where their digestive system cannot digest some foods. Foods that can cause intolerance include milk, eggs, and yeast.

Tip: If eating certain foods causes an unwanted reaction, such as feeling bloated, see a doctor.

Vitamins and minerals

A number of vitamins and minerals must be included in the diet. A deficiency, or lack, of any of these can cause illness. The specific illness depends on the role of the nutrient in the body.

Nutrient	Needed for	Illness caused by deficiency
calcium	strong bones	osteoporosis, rickets
iron	red blood cells	anemia
vitamin A	eyes, skin, bones	night blindness, dry skin, blindness in children
vitamins B1 and B2	nerves, digesting carbohydrates	mouth ulcers, pellagra, beriberi
vitamin B12	nerve function, red blood cells	anemia, loss of concentration
vitamin C	mucus membranes, blood clotting	scurvy
vitamin K	blood clotting	excessive bleeding from wounds

Diagnosing problems

Doctors who treat digestive problems are called gastroenterologists. These experts can diagnose many problems by asking patients about their diet and bowel habits. They can use medical imaging tools to look inside the body and see what is happening. Modern medical imaging tools allow doctors to treat many problems without surgery.

Endoscopy

An endoscopy is a procedure that uses a miniature camera, called an endoscope. The endoscope is inserted into the patient to examine the inside of the digestive system. In this simple procedure, doctors can examine and diagnose problems in parts of the body that are otherwise hidden.

FASCINATING FACT

Some people have allergic reactions to particular foods. Peanuts, for instance, can cause breathing problems and even kill some people. It is important that these people are aware of the foods that cause them problems. They must be ready with first aid if exposed to these foods.

The surgeon views the images taken by the endoscope on a large screen.

Ulcers

Ulcers are among the most common digestive tract problems. Many people suffer from mouth ulcers, but far more serious ulcers can occur in the stomach and intestines. A doctor may diagnose these from listening to the patient's symptoms, or they may be found during an endoscope examination.

Ulcers form when the inner layers of the stomach or intestines (mucosa and submucosa) become damaged and eroded. Ulcers are particularly painful in the stomach because of the stomach acid. A layer of mucus secreted by the stomach lining normally protects the stomach wall from acid. An ulcer allows the acid to touch the stomach wall.

Drugs are very successful in treating ulcers, but sometimes surgery is needed. The cause of ulcers in many cases in unclear. Scientists now know that a bacterium called *Helicobactor pylori* is involved in many cases.

Stomach ulcers UNDER THE MICROSCOPE

A stomach ulcer (red) can erode the layer of mucosa (rough texture around the ulcer).

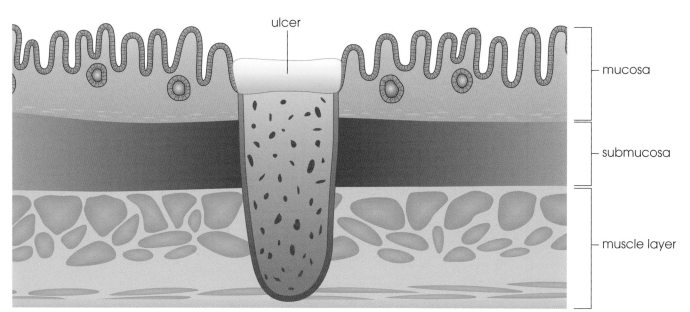

A severe ulcer can eat through many layers in the wall of the stomach.

Taking care of digestion

The easiest way to look after your digestive system is to listen to what it tells you. Eat when you are hungry, go to the toilet when your body feels the need. Make sure you have enough water and be sensible about what you eat by limiting special food treats. Maintain healthy behaviors, such as washing your hands before eating, and taking the time to enjoy your food.

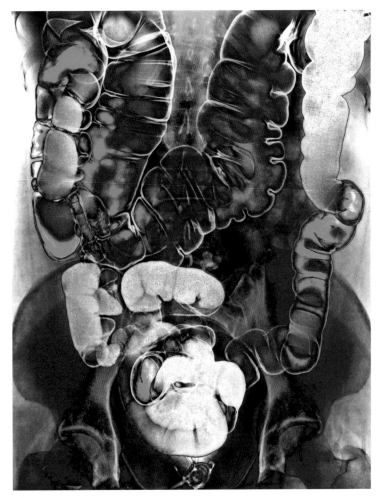

This X ray shows a healthy large intestine.

The role of fiber

Having sufficient **fiber** in the diet can help the large intestine to work better. Fiber makes the contents of the large intestine softer and more bulky and easier to pass through the bowel. Fiber may also protect the bowel against some diseases, such as bowel cancers.

+

HEALTH TIP
Healthy variety

People used to eat a greater variety of foods, particularly fruits and vegetables. A diet that is lacking in variety can limit your vitamin and mineral intake.

Tip: Try different foods. Eat at least seven different vegetables every day.

Food preparation

Learning to prepare food for yourself can help you to enjoy a variety of foods. When preparing food, follow these simple rules of hygiene:

- wash your hands before and after handling food
- wash counters and use clean utensils and dishes
- cook meat thoroughly
- store foods correctly

In case of poisoning

Food poisoning can be caused by bacteria in food or by consuming chemicals. Treatment will depend on the cause of the problem. If you suffer food poisoning you should:

- stay off solid foods for 24 hours after vomiting ceases
- rest and drink plenty of water
- seek medical assistance

Be prepared

It is important to be prepared in the event of chemical poisoning. Have a chart ready with first aid treatments, including specific treatments for different chemical poisons. If you are not sure what to do, contact emergency services. In the United States, emergency services are contacted by dialing 911.

Always use clean cutlery when preparing food.

ACTIVITY Taste and smell test

The nose plays an important role in tasting food. Explore this by tasting a range of foods with and without your sense of smell.

You will need

- a range of raw fruit and vegetables, cut into small pieces
- toothpicks
- a glass of water

What to do

1 Blindfold your partner and have them block their nose firmly. Using a toothpick, feed them one piece of food at a time. Make sure they drink a mouthful of water between each tasting. Can they guess what the food is?

2 Try the test again without having the nose blocked. How well can they identify the foods now?

Explanation

Smell signals reach the brain more quickly than the taste signals. Often it is actually the smell of food that you "taste."

Glossary

abdomen	the area below the chest
bacteria	microscopic living things, some of which cause disease
carbohydrates	nutrients found in bread and fruits, which provide energy for the body
cells	the smallest units of living things
diarrhea	runny or frequent bowel motions
digestive organs	the organs and glands that produce digestive juices
digestive tract	the parts of the digestive system that food passes through
enzymes	chemicals that assist in breaking down food
fiber	tough food matter found in whole grains, fruit, and vegetables
genetic disorder	disorder that is inherited, or passed on in a family from one generation to the next
insulin	a substance produced by the pancreas that helps control blood sugar levels
micro-organisms	microscopic living things, such as bacteria
molecules	the smallest units of a substance
mucus	watery fluid produced by the walls of the stomach and intestines
nutrients	chemicals the body needs to grow and stay healthy
peristalsis	movement of the muscles in the oesophagus walls that pushes bolus down to the stomach
protein	a nutrient found in meat, fish, and eggs, which is needed for developing many body structures
starches	types of food that break down into sugars
tissues	groups of similar cells that make up the fabric of body systems
ulcer	an eroded area in the lining of the stomach or intestines

Index